Armenia
 Australia
 Austria
 **Azerbaijan**
 **Bahamas**
 Bahrain
 Bangladesh

 **Bosnia-Herzegovina**
 Botswana
 Brazil
 **Brunei**
 Bulgaria
Burkina Faso
Burma (Myanmar)

 Chile
 China
 Colombia
 Comoros
 Congo
 Congo (Democratic Republic)
 Costa Rica

 Dominican Republic
 East Timor
 **Ecuador**
 Egypt
 El Salvador
 Equatorial Guinea
Eritrea

 Georgia
 Germany
 **Ghana**
 Greece
 Greenland
 Grenada
 Guatemala

 India
 Indonesia
 **Iran**
 Iraq
 **Ireland**
 Israel
 Italy

 Korea, North
 **Korea, South**
 Kosovo
 **Kuwait**
 **Kyrgyzstan**
 Laos
 **Latvia**

PHILIP'S
Infant School
Atlas

DAVID WRIGHT AND RACHEL NOONAN

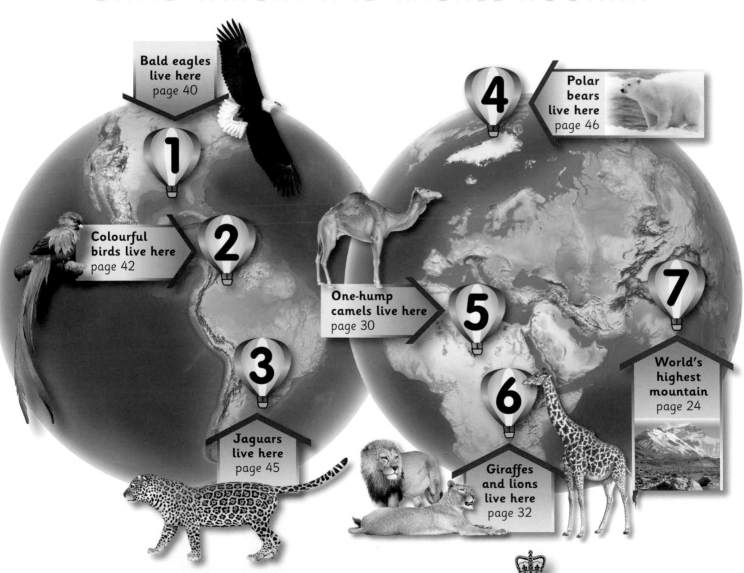

Bald eagles live here page 40

1

Colourful birds live here page 42

2

Jaguars live here page 45

3

Polar bears live here page 46

4

One-hump camels live here page 30

5

Giraffes and lions live here page 32

6

World's highest mountain page 24

7

IN ASSOCIATION WITH
THE ROYAL GEOGRAPHICAL SOCIETY
WITH THE INSTITUTE OF BRITISH GEOGRAPHERS

About this Atlas

Message to Adults

Children love discovering new things ... this atlas has hundreds of new things to discover! Some will even be a surprise for adults!

This is an atlas for young children to enjoy. We can't tell children everything about everywhere, but we *can* take them to some amazing places.

They will find out a lot about the geography, people, climate, plants and animals – as well as some of the problems – of our amazing world!

Don't worry about detailed understanding just yet. The numbered balloons on the maps allow the children to find the places on each map. Every numbered balloon has a corresponding picture and text about that particular *real* place.

As well as beautiful photographs and illustrations, we have included lots of wonderful postage stamps: real messages from real places! There are messages on the flags we have chosen too.

Message to Children

Welcome to this world atlas – let's explore the world together!

Our **balloon** takes you to **real places**. You can find where these places are on the **maps**. The **pictures** and **words** tell you more about each place.

You will soon discover things that most grown-ups don't know!

Meet the Authors

Both the authors are graduates who have travelled round the world. David has been to 106 countries! He was a university lecturer, and now he is an author: he has written 20 books.

His daughter Rachel works with children at her local school in Norwich, UK, where her 3 children go to school.

When you've visited all the places in this atlas, you can meet David again and find out more about our world in **Philip's Children's Atlas**, written for 7 to 12 year olds by David and his wife Jill.

David Wright

Rachel Noonan

First published in Great Britain in 2009 by Philip's, a division of Octopus Publishing Group Limited (www.octopusbooks.co.uk)
Endeavour House, 189 Shaftesbury Avenue, London WC2H 8JY
An Hachette UK Company (www.hachette.co.uk)

To Florence, Molly and Isaac
Text © 2009 David Wright and Rachel Noonan
Maps © 2009 Philip's
Reprinted 2010 (twice), 2012 (with revisions), 2013, 2014

Cartography by Philip's

A CIP catalogue record for this book is available from the British Library.

ISBN 978–0–540–09121–8

David Wright and Rachel Noonan have asserted their moral rights under the Copyright, Designs and Patents Act, 1988, to be identified as the authors of this work.

Printed in Hong Kong

Details of other Philip's titles and services can be found on our website at: **www.philips-maps.co.uk**

Contents

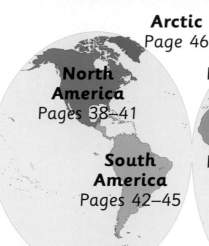

Arctic
Page 46

Europe
Pages 12–19

Asia
Pages 20–29

North
America
Pages 38–41

Africa
Pages 30–33

South
America
Pages 42–45

Pacific
Pages 34–37

Antarctica
Page 47

Our Planet Earth

Our Planet in Space   4–5
Our Planet Earth is ...   6–7
Understanding Maps   8–9
Oceans, Continents and Countries   10–11

Europe – Discover...

... the British Isles   12–13
... Western Europe   14–15
... Mediterranean Europe   16–17
... Eastern Europe   18–19

Asia – Discover...

... Russia and its Neighbours   20–21
... the Middle East   22–23
... India and Southern Asia   24–25
... Southeast Asia   26–27
... China and its Neighbours   28–29

Africa – Discover...

... North and West Africa   30–31
... Central and Southern Africa   32–33

The Pacific – Discover...

... the Pacific   34–35
... Australia and New Zealand   36–37

North America – Discover...

... Canada and Alaska   38–39
... the USA   40–41

South America – Discover...

... Central America   42–43
... South America   44–45

Polar Regions – Discover...

... the Arctic   46
... Antarctica   47

Index and Answers to Questions   48
Glossary   49

Philip's and the Royal Geographical Society

This Philip's atlas displays the logo of the **Royal Geographical Society** (with the **Institute of British Geographers**). The Royal Geographical Society supports education, teaching, research and expeditions. The role of 'promoting public understanding of geography' now reaches 5 to 7 year olds through this new atlas.

Philip's has been publishing good maps for over 150 years.

Find out more about the Royal Geographical Society! Visit their website at www.rgs.org – David Wright is a Fellow and a Chartered Geographer of the RGS.

Our Planet in Space

Space is huge! This picture shows the **planets** in our **Solar System**. These planets go round our Sun. But if you look at the sky at night you can see hundreds of **stars**. The stars you see are mostly other suns far, far away.

Sun

Mercury

Venus

Earth

Mars

Jupiter

Saturn

Uranus

Neptune

How long does it take for the planets to go round the Sun? They are all different. **Earth** takes **365 days** (1 year). **Mercury** only takes **88 Earth-days**, but **Neptune** takes **165 Earth-years** to circle the Sun!

Did you know?

The planets of the Solar System are very different sizes, and the Sun is huge! If the **Sun** was the size of a basketball then **Jupiter** (the biggest planet) would be the size of a pea, and the **Earth** would be smaller than a full stop!

8 planets circle the Sun. How can you remember the planets? Here is a funny sentence to help you. Can you think of an even funnier sentence to help you remember the order of the planets, using the first letter of each planet?

Mercury	My	M..........
Venus	Very	V..........
Earth	Excellent	E..........
Mars	Mother	M..........
Jupiter	Just	J..........
Saturn	Served	S..........
Uranus	Us	U..........
Neptune	Noodles	N..........

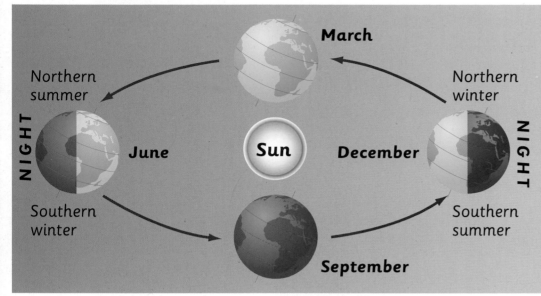

Winter is when our part of the Earth is **tilted away from the Sun**, and gets **less sunlight** and **heat**. **Summer** is when our part of the Earth is **tilted to get more sunlight** and **heat**. Tropical lands get the most heat from the Sun; Arctic lands get the least heat.

Can you be the Earth going round the Sun?
Use a ball. Spin it all the way round. This is one day. Now get a friend to stand still – they can be the Sun. Walk all the way round your friend spinning the world **365 times**!
This is one year!

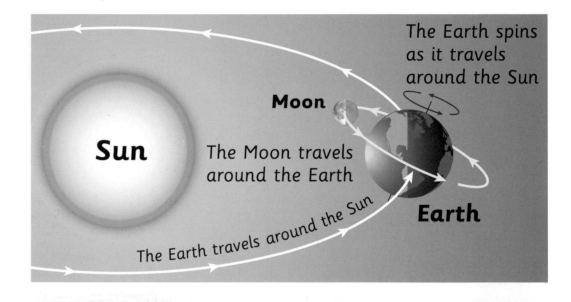

The Earth spins as it travels around the Sun

Moon

The Moon travels around the Earth

The Earth travels around the Sun

Sun

Earth

Our planet is so beautiful!
Can you find where **YOU** live? Find the names of the continents on pages 10–11.

What makes Earth such a GOOD planet to live on?
The **Sun** makes us warm. We've got **land** to live on. We've got **soil** for crops. We've got **air** to breathe. We've got **water** to drink. We've got **coal**, **oil**, **sun** and **wind** for energy. We've got **friends** too! Can you think of more good reasons to live here?

Our Planet Earth is ...

1 ... so beautiful!

Imagine you are in a spacecraft; you look out of the window and see **THIS!**

Wow! You can see blue **oceans**, white **clouds** and green **land**.

2 ... so varied

Our artist has put 4 amazing places on 1 picture!
Can you find...

... cold, icy Antarctica (find out more on page **47**),
... hot, sandy desert (see page **30**),
... tall fir forest by a lake (see page **20**),
... a city with skyscrapers (see page **29**)?

CAN YOU FIND...
North America? (Find out more on page **38**.)
South America? (See page **44**.)
Some islands? (See page **43**.)

3 ... a sphere

An easy shape to understand. If you've caught a ball, you know the shape of our planet! (See page **4**.)

4 ... so light – and so dark!

In one whole year every place on Earth has **equal time in light and darkness** – half and half. [**It's true!**]

JUNE

North

NIGHT

16 hours of daylight

12 hours of daylight

Equator

8 hours of daylight

South

SUN'S RAYS

DECEMBER

8 hours of daylight

North

12 hours of daylight

NIGHT

Equator

16 hours of daylight

South

It is so easy to work out the shortest routes for aeroplanes!

To find the shortest route by air on a globe:

1 Find your start point (**A**).

2 Find your end point (**B**).

3 Put a piece of string between your start point and end point.

4 Pull the string tight – and that's the shortest route!

Surprise! From **London** (**A**) to **Los Angeles** (**B**), the shortest route goes over **Greenland**!

A

B

ATLANTIC OCEAN

But it is so difficult to put the world on a flat map!

Find out more on page **8**. This stamp from **Canada** shows one way of keeping shapes right – do you like it?

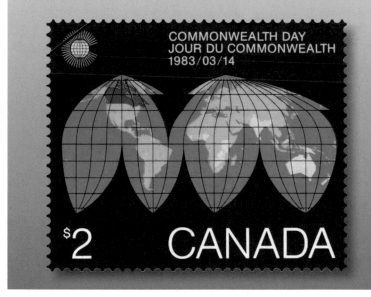

COMMONWEALTH DAY
JOUR DU COMMONWEALTH
1983/03/14

$2 CANADA

But – we pollute our planet in lots of ways.

We put rubbish on the **land** and in the **sea**.

We pollute the **air**.

We spoil our **soils**.

We cut down **trees**.

We catch too many **fish**.

Understanding Maps

The best way to understand maps is to **USE maps!**

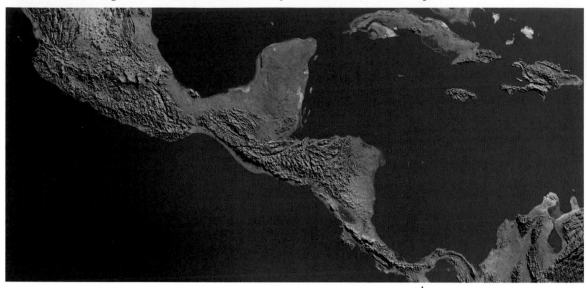

This is a **SATELLITE IMAGE** of Central America. ↑

This is a **MAP** of Central America. ↑

Here is an image taken from a satellite in space. Look at the image and the map. Can you find: the **land**, the **sea**, **islands**, a **lake**, and some **mountains**?

Here is a map of the same places. **Can you spot some differences?** A map is like a picture taken from the air. A map can tell you a lot more than a picture: the names of cities, rivers and mountains, and borders where countries begin and end.

The satellite image does not show any borders.
Can you see which **map colour** is used for the **sea** and the **rivers**?*
Can you see which **map colour** is used for **borders**?*

Maps can be of very big places, or of small places.
Can you draw a map of your bedroom? A globe is a map of the whole world. Maps are usually flat, but a **globe** is a map and it is a **sphere**!

What can maps tell us?

Blue is for water

★ Red star is for capital cities

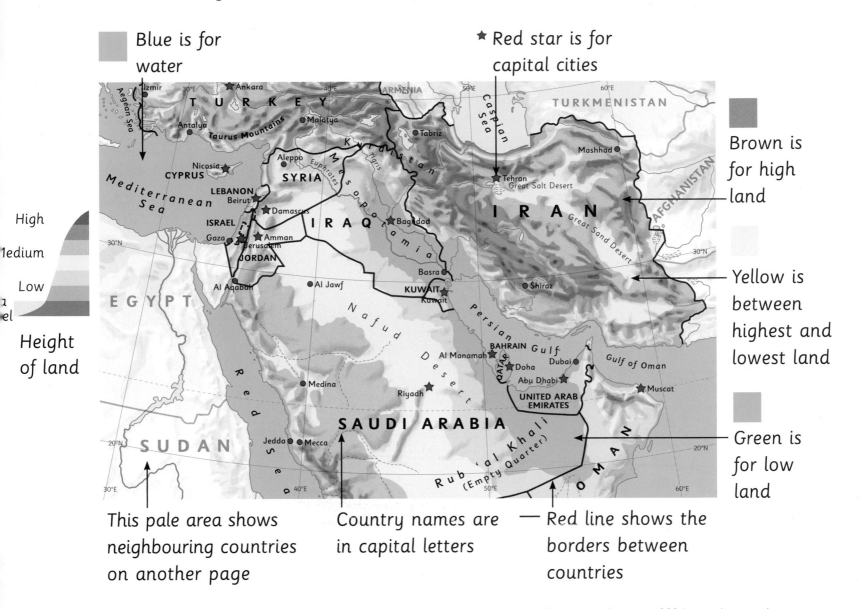

Brown is for high land

Yellow is between highest and lowest land

High

Medium

Low

Height of land

Green is for low land

This pale area shows neighbouring countries on another page

Country names are in capital letters

— Red line shows the borders between countries

This is the scale bar. It tells you how far **1 centimetre** on the map is on the real world!

Scale 1:22,000,000   1 cm on the map = 220 km on the ground

| 0 | 220 km | 500 km | | 1,000 km | | 1,500 km | | 2,000 km |

Where in the world?

This little map of the world is on every page. It shows you where in the world the big map is. It also shows you how big that bit of the world is. **Use a globe as well!** Only globes always have the right size and the right shape for all parts of the world.

Map makers

(cartographers) are so careful to make maps accurate that you can even use a map to find out how far it is from one place to another place.

Oceans, Continents and Countries

This map shows our whole world.

Our 7 continents are named in big, bold letters like this: **EUROPE**.
Our world has **4 oceans** – can you name them? A..., A..., I..., and P....
The **'Top 10' countries** are named on this map. These countries have the most people.

Find the **blue** people with **white** numbers. China has the most people, so is number 1. India is 2, USA is 3 and so on. Most of the 'Top 10' are in Asia, but can you find ...

ONE in **North America**?*
[This is easy!]
ONE in **South America**?*
ONE in **Africa**?*

'TOP 10' COUNTRIES:

1. **China** 1,314 million people
2. **India** 1,095 million people
3. **USA** 298 million people
4. **Indonesia** 245 million people
5. **Brazil** 188 million people
6. **Pakistan** 166 million people
7. **Bangladesh** 147 million people
8. **Russia** 143 million people
9. **Nigeria** 132 million people
10. **Japan** 127 million people

A stamp from Switzerland. This is the badge of the United Nations.

The **Atlantic Ocean** is **7 times bigger** than the **Arctic Ocean**.

The **Pacific Ocean** is **HUGE! GIGANTIC! ENORMOUS!** It is bigger than **ALL** the world's land!

NATIONS UNIES
HELVETIA
50

CANADA
NORTH AMERICA
USA
PACIFIC OCEAN
ATLANTIC OCEAN
BRAZIL
SOUTH AMERICA
ANTARCTICA

Arctic Circle
Tropic of Cancer
Equator
Tropic of Capricorn
Antarctic Circle

The 'BIG 6' countries.

① ② ③ ④ ⑤ ⑥

There are 6 very big countries – our map shows them all. We can all see the biggest country: **Russia!** It is over 17 million square kilometres in area.

'BIG 6': a list of all the countries with more than 4 million square kilometres of land.

① Russia Over 17 million
② Canada Nearly 10 million
③ USA Over 9 million
④ China Over 9 million
⑤ Brazil Over 8 million
⑥ Australia Over 7 million

The 'snip' at the bottom of the map allows continents to be the right **SIZE** and the right **SHAPE**. Many world maps make the cold lands too **BIG** and the hot lands too **SMALL**. Our map gets it right!

A stamp from Fiji. The Pacific Ocean is in the middle!

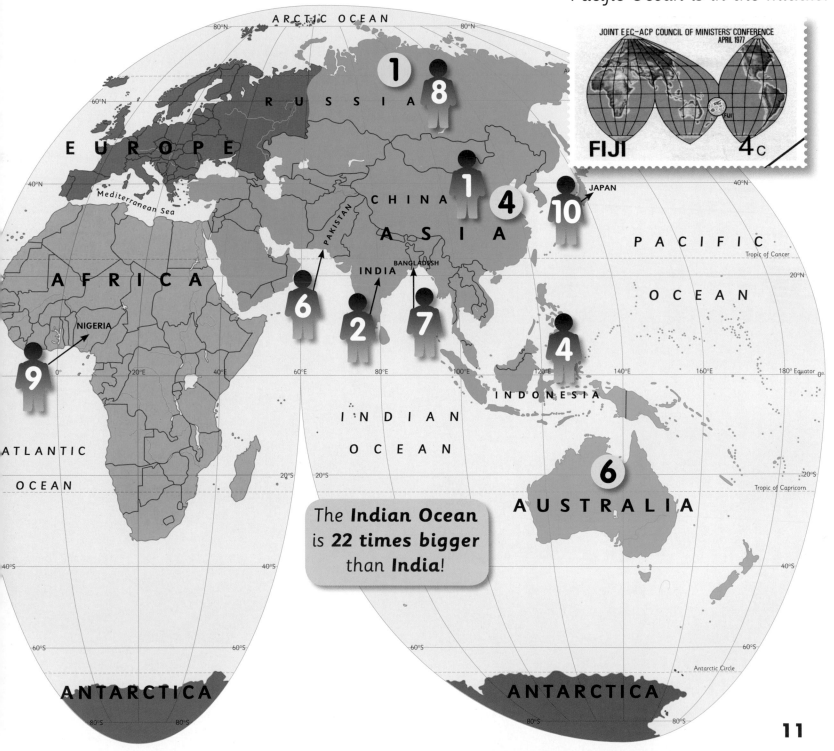

JOINT EEC–ACP COUNCIL OF MINISTERS' CONFERENCE APRIL 1977

FIJI   4c

ARCTIC OCEAN

RUSSIA

EUROPE

Mediterranean Sea

CHINA

PAKISTAN

ASIA

JAPAN

PACIFIC

OCEAN

Tropic of Cancer

AFRICA

INDIA

BANGLADESH

NIGERIA

ATLANTIC

OCEAN

INDIAN

OCEAN

INDONESIA

AUSTRALIA

Tropic of Capricorn

The **Indian Ocean is 22 times bigger** than **India!**

ANTARCTICA

ANTARCTICA

Antarctic Circle

11

Discover... the British Isles

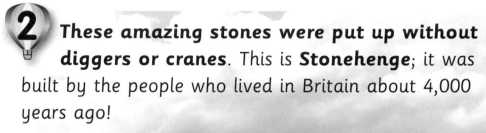

1 Can you see the houses of Parliament and Big Ben? This is where the government of the United Kingdom meets to make new laws.

This giant wheel takes you up, so that you can see London from the air.

2 **These amazing stones were put up without diggers or cranes**. This is **Stonehenge**; it was built by the people who lived in Britain about 4,000 years ago!

3 **This is a little train for big people!** Now it carries tourists, but it used to carry slate. **100 years ago** there was a lot of mining in **Wales**. Welsh slate makes really good roofs.

4 **This bridge is so amazing!** This picture is on a £1 coin! It was built for trains by the Victorians over 100 years ago. The **Forth Bridge** was the first big bridge made of steel.

6 This cross is special. It is an old Celtic cross in **Ireland**. Can you draw the pattern carved on it?

5 **Scotland** has big mountains and great wildlife. This is **Ben Nevis**, the highest mountain in the British Isles. **Can you** see what the osprey will have for dinner?

To the
North Pole
page 46

Did you know?
The Shetland Islands are much nearer to **NORWAY** than to London! (See map on page 15.)

The Union Jack...

England + Scotland + St Patrick

...is made from **THREE FLAGS**!

This way
to Canada
page 39

This way
to Western
Europe
page 15

7 **The flag of Ireland:**
Green for Catholics;
Orange for Protestants;
and White in the middle
for peace in Ireland.

This way to the
Mediterranean
page 17

Scale 1:5,500,000   1 cm on the map = 55 km on the ground

0   55 km   100 km   200 km   300 km   400 km   500 km

ATLANTIC OCEAN

Shetland Islands
Lerwick

Orkney Islands
Kirkwall

Cape Wrath
Thurso

Lewis
Stornoway

St Kilda

Outer Hebrides

North West Highlands
Inverness
Aviemore
Aberdeen

Portree
Skye

Inner Hebrides

Fort William
Ben Nevis

SCOTLAND
Dundee

Mull
Oban

Stirling
Edinburgh
Firth of Forth
Berwick-upon-Tweed

Glasgow
Clyde

Arran

Southern Uplands

Dumfries
Carlisle
Newcastle-upon-Tyne
Tyne

UNITED KINGDOM

Londonderry
NORTHERN IRELAND
North Channel
Belfast

Donegal

Sligo

Isle of Man
Douglas

Scarborough

Pennines

York
Leeds
Blackpool

IRELAND

Galway
Dublin

Irish Sea
Anglesey

Liverpool
Manchester
Sheffield
Lincoln

ENGLAND

Shannon
Limerick

Wrexham
Nottingham
Shrewsbury
Leicester
Norwich

Wexford

Aberystwyth WALES
Birmingham

Killarney

Severn
Cambridge
Ipswich

Cork

Brecon
Gloucester
Oxford
London

Carmarthen
Swansea
Thames

Cardiff
Bristol
Salisbury

Hastings

Exeter
Portsmouth
Isle of Wight

Plymouth

FRANCE

Penzance
Truro

Isles of Scilly

English Channel

North Sea

Discover...
Western Europe

1 Over 1,000 years ago the Vikings sailed from Norway. Viking boats were amazing. People could sail them, row them and even carry them! Vikings sailed to many lands.

2 Reindeer live in the far north. The far north of Europe is inside the **Arctic Circle**. Find out more on page 46.

3 Why do people decorate trees at Christmas? The tradition of Christmas trees came from **Germany**. Now Christians all over the world decorate trees in their homes at Christmas time – the 'birthday' of Jesus.

4 The European Union has its head office in Belgium. SURPRISE! The walls are made of ... **GLASS**!

What is this flag? This is the flag of the **EU** – the **European Union**. Find more EU countries on pages 17 and 19. People travel from all over Europe to **Belgium** to discuss new ideas and laws.

5 The Arc de Triomphe is in Paris, the capital of France. The words mean 'triumphal arch'. It lists the victories of Emperor Napoleon.

6 Skiing is fun in the Alps in winter. The high snowy mountains of Switzerland make good ski slopes in winter.

Scale 1:17,500,000   1 cm on the map = 175 km on the ground

To the North Pole
page 46

This way to Russia
page 21

This way to USA
page 41

To Africa
page 31

ATLANTIC OCEAN

ICELAND
Reykjavik

Norwegian Sea

Faroe Islands

Shetland Islands

Orkney Islands

Hebrides

Inverness
Aberdeen
Glasgow   Edinburgh

North Sea

Belfast
IRELAND
Dublin
Limerick
Cork

UNITED KINGDOM
Manchester
Birmingham
Cardiff
London
Plymouth

English Channel
Channel Islands

Bay of Biscay

Bordeaux

FRANCE

Toulouse

Pyrenees

PORTUGAL

SPAIN

Tromso

Lapland

RUSSIA

FINLAND
Kokkola
Helsinki

RUSSIA
ESTONIA
LATVIA
LITHUANIA
RUSSIA
BELARUS

Trondheim

Bergen
Oslo
Stockholm

Baltic Sea

DENMARK   Copenhagen

Hamburg
NETHERLANDS
Amsterdam
Berlin

POLAND

BELGIUM   Brussels   Bonn
Luxembourg
LUXEMBOURG

GERMANY
Frankfurt

CZECH REPUBLIC

UKRAINE

SLOVAK REPUBLIC

Seine   Paris
Strasbourg
Rhine
Munich
Danube   Vienna
Salzburg
AUSTRIA

HUNGARY

Berne
SWITZERLAND
LIECHTENSTEIN

Geneva

Rhone

Avignon
Nice
Marseilles

Corsica

ITALY

SLOVENIA
CROATIA
BOSNIA-HERZEGOVINA
SERBIA

Adriatic Sea

MONTENEGRO
KOSOVO
ALBANIA
MACEDONIA

ROMANIA

Tyrrhenian Sea

Ionian Sea

GREECE

Mediterranean Sea

MOROCCO
ALGERIA
TUNISIA
MALTA

Barents Sea

15

Discover...
Mediterranean Europe

1 **A procession to remember Jesus in Burgos.**
The days before Easter in **Spain** are called **Semana Santa** (Holy Week). There are processions every day. People feel sad but on Easter Day everyone feels happy again.

2 **This is the flag of Slovenia:** the shield shows the three peaks of Mount Triglav.

3 **The Colosseum in Rome.** Lots of buildings in **Rome** were built by the Romans over **2,000 years ago**. Now millions of people live here, so there are lots of new buildings and cars too.

4 **This is a new bridge that looks old.** The old bridge was blown up in the war in **Bosnia** in 1993. Now there is peace – and the bridge has been built again, just like the old bridge.

5 This temple is over **2,000 years old.** It is called the **Parthenon**. It is in **Athens**, the capital city of Greece. How many columns can you count? Do you know any words that come from Greek words? Clue: find words with 'ph': they come from Greece!

6 What is growing here? These are **olive trees** in Crete. Olives and grapes grow well in Mediterranean lands. Why? Remember the 5 Ws: '**Warm Wet Westerly Winds** in **Winter**'.

7 There are lots of fish in the Mediterranean Sea. Fish is good food and tourists like to eat fish. But there are two problems: over-fishing and pollution. This photo shows a fish shop in **Naples**, **Italy**.

Scale 1:15,000,000 1 cm on the map = 150 km on the ground

| 0 | 150 km | 500 km | 1,000 km | 1,500 km | 2,000 km |

| 0 | 1 | 2 | 3 | 4 cm 5 | 6 | 7 | 8 | 9 cm 10 | 11 | 12 | 13 |

This way to the USA page 41

This way to Russia page 21

Discover...
Eastern Europe

1 **This looks like hard work!** This horse is pulling a plough in **Poland**; the farmer is keeping it straight. Soon there will be good cabbages to eat. Try looking for Polish food in shops – can you find **pierogi** or **golagki**?

2 **Which ALPHABET or АЛФАВИТ?**
Belarus and Ukraine use the Russian Cyrillic alphabet. Try writing your name using the key below!

3 **Children in Ukraine** are folk-dancing. It's fun – and a good way to find out about history.
Did you know? Ukraine is bigger than France!

4 **Skiers catch this train**. They travel through snowy forests to the Carpathian Mountains in the **Slovak Republic**.

А	Б	В	Г	Д	Е	Ё	Ж	З	И	Й	К	Л	М	Н	О	П	Р	С	Т	У	Ф	Х	Ц	Ч	Ш	Щ	Ю	Я
A	B	V	G	D	E	YO	ZH	Z	I	Y	K	L	M	N	O	P	R	S	T	U	F	KH	TS	CH	SH	SHCH	YU	YA

1987

Today

Spot the differences!

Lots of the countries of Eastern Europe were not on the map in 1987. Can you find some?

Spot **6** new countries* – **well done!**

Spot **8** – **excellent!**

Spot **10** – **FANTASTIC!**

5 **The River Danube passes through 8 countries.**

It flows from Germany to the Black Sea. This boat **pushes** big barges.

Scale 1:16,000,000   1 cm on the map = 160 km on the ground

0   160 km   500 km   1,000 km   1,500 km   2,000 km

This way to the Arctic page 46

Can you find 2 big seas beginning with B?*

This way to Russia page 21

To Africa page 31

Discover... the Middle East

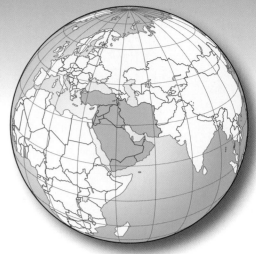

The Dome of the Rock is an Islamic monument. Before that there was probably a Christian church and before that a Roman temple and a Jewish temple.

1 **Jerusalem means 'Place of Peace'.** It is a holy city for 3 big religions: Islam, Judaism and Christianity.

Religion	Symbol	Holy day
Islam	☪	Friday
Judaism	✡	Saturday
Christianity	✝	Sunday

2 **Petra in Jordan was once a 'lost city'.** Now the ruins are visited by thousands of people! **Amazing!** This temple was carved out of solid rock!

Did you know?

The Middle East is the only place where **3 continents** meet. Can you name them?* The map on page 23 will help you.

3 **Iraq has old and new ruins.** The old ruins are from some of the oldest cities on Earth! The new ruins are from wars.

4 Muslims all over the world pray facing Mecca. One of the 5 pillars of Islam is to pray 5 times a day; another is to visit Mecca at least once.

5 Much of the Middle East is very dry, so irrigating (watering) the land is very important. This stamp from **Oman** shows an irrigation channel. What else can you see in the picture?*

SULTANATE OF OMAN
130 BAISA
INTERNATIONAL ENVIRONMENT DAY

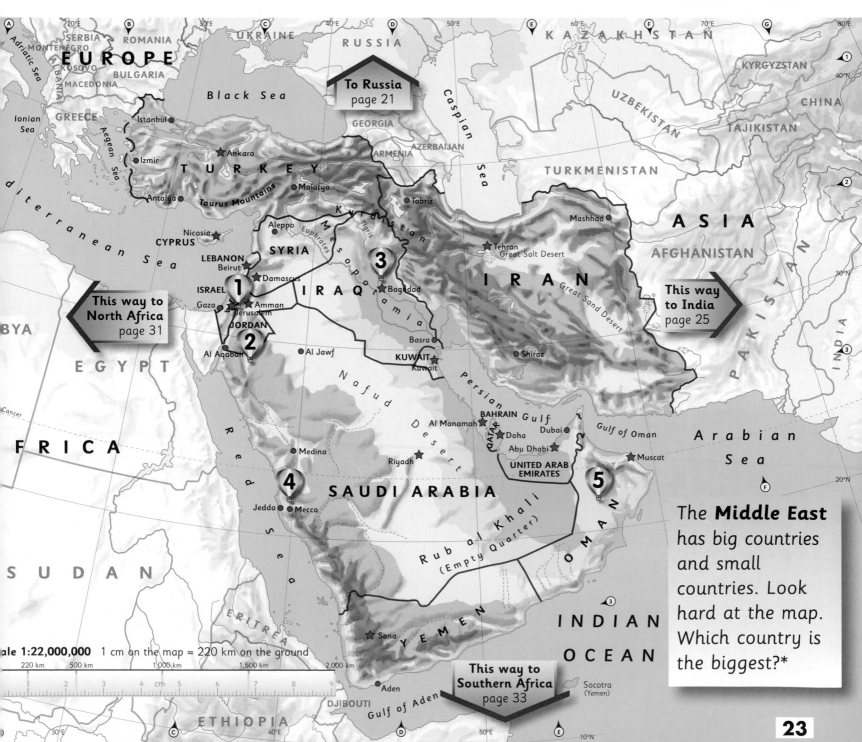

To Russia
page 21

This way to North Africa
page 31

This way to India
page 25

This way to Southern Africa
page 33

The **Middle East** has big countries and small countries. Look hard at the map. Which country is the biggest?*

Scale 1:22,000,000   1 cm on the map = 220 km on the ground
220 km   500 km   1,000 km   1,500 km   2,000 km

Discover...
India and Southern Asia

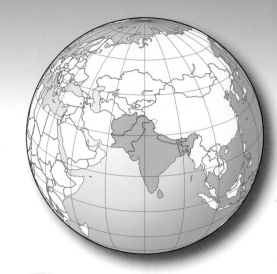

1 **Afghanistan has high mountains, dry deserts and lonely ruins.**
But wars have made it a very hard place to live in.

Did you know?
3 religions started in India – **Hinduism**, **Sikhism** and **Buddhism**. Lots of different languages are spoken in India – and many of them have their own alphabet. **Islam** is the main religion in Afghanistan, Pakistan and Bangladesh.

2 **Pakistan is mostly desert**, yet it has more people than any country in Europe or Africa. How can so many people live here? The **River Indus** brings water all year from the high mountains.

POSTAGE PAISA **10** PAKISTAN
RICE WE EXPORT THE BEST
পাকিস্তান

4 **Yaks are amazing animals!**
People come to the Himalayas to climb the highest mountains in the world. Yaks help to carry all the things the people need. All yaks need is water, grass and their thick fur!

3 **This is the Taj Mahal.**
Over 1,000 elephants were used to bring stone to build this beautiful building.

6 In Sri Lanka, tea grows in high mountains – where the days are hot and the nights are cold. Tea-pickers take 2 leaves from each stalk and put them in the baskets on their backs.

5 **Mumbai (Bombay) is a big city.** Some people here are rich, but many are very poor.

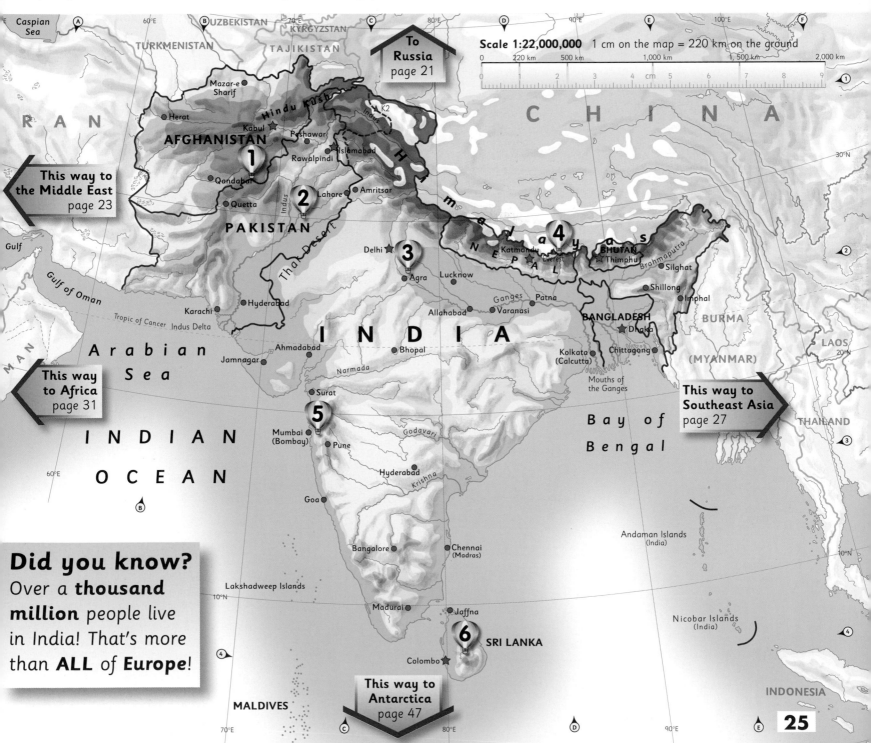

Scale 1:22,000,000   1 cm on the map = 220 km on the ground

0   220 km   500 km   1,000 km   1,500 km   2,000 km

To Russia page 21

This way to the Middle East page 23

This way to Africa page 31

This way to Southeast Asia page 27

Did you know? Over a **thousand million** people live in India! That's more than **ALL** of Europe!

This way to Antarctica page 47

MALDIVES

Caspian Sea

UZBEKISTAN

KYRGYZSTAN

TURKMENISTAN

TAJIKISTAN

CHINA

IRAN

Herat

Hindu Kush

K2

Mazar-e Sharif

Kabul

Peshawar

Islamabad

AFGHANISTAN

Rawalpindi

Qandahar

Lahore

Amritsar

Quetta

PAKISTAN

Indus

Thar Desert

Delhi

Agra

Lucknow

NEPAL

Katmandu

Everest

BHUTAN

Thimphu

Brahmaputra

Silghat

Shillong

Imphal

Gulf

Gulf of Oman

Karachi

Hyderabad

Tropic of Cancer

Indus Delta

Ganges

Allahabad

Varanasi

Patna

BANGLADESH

Dhaka

BURMA (MYANMAR)

LAOS

Arabian Sea

Ahmadabad

INDIA

Bhopal

Narmada

Kolkata (Calcutta)

Chittagong

Jamnagar

Jaffna

Mouths of the Ganges

Surat

Mumbai (Bombay)

Pune

Godavari

Bay of Bengal

THAILAND

INDIAN OCEAN

Hyderabad

Krishna

Goa

Bangalore

Chennai (Madras)

Andaman Islands (India)

Lakshadweep Islands

Madurai

Jaffna

Nicobar Islands (India)

SRI LANKA

Colombo

INDONESIA

Discover...
Southeast Asia

Rice is planted in flooded fields. But water runs down hills! So – how do you grow rice on a slope? Look at Balloon 6 for a clue.

2 **A beautiful palace in Bangkok**, the capital city of Thailand. How many spires can you count?

3 **This is the flag of Cambodia.** In the centre is a drawing of the temple of Angkor Wat.

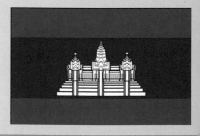

4 **Fishing in Vietnam** – these round fishing boats are in the South China Sea. Fish is good food, but too much fishing causes too few fish.

1 **In Burma many boys become Buddhist monks.** Sometimes they join for a few weeks, sometimes for their whole lives. They wear special clothes, like the boy in this picture. People respect monks and are happy to give them food.

5 Where does rubber come from?

This is a rubber tree in a plantation in **Malaysia**. The rubber is the sap of the tree. Some can be 'tapped' and collected.

GETAH
Hevea brasiliensis
WILAYAH PERSEKUTUAN
Malaysia 15¢

6 Can you see where people have cut steps into the hill?

These are flat places (called terraces) to plant rice and hold the water. This means that lots of rice can be grown even on steep slopes.

Scale 1:25,000,000   1 cm on the map = 250 km on the ground

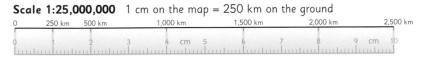

0   250 km   500 km   1,000 km   1,500 km   2,000 km   2,500 km
0   1   2   3   4   cm   5   6   7   8   9   cm   10

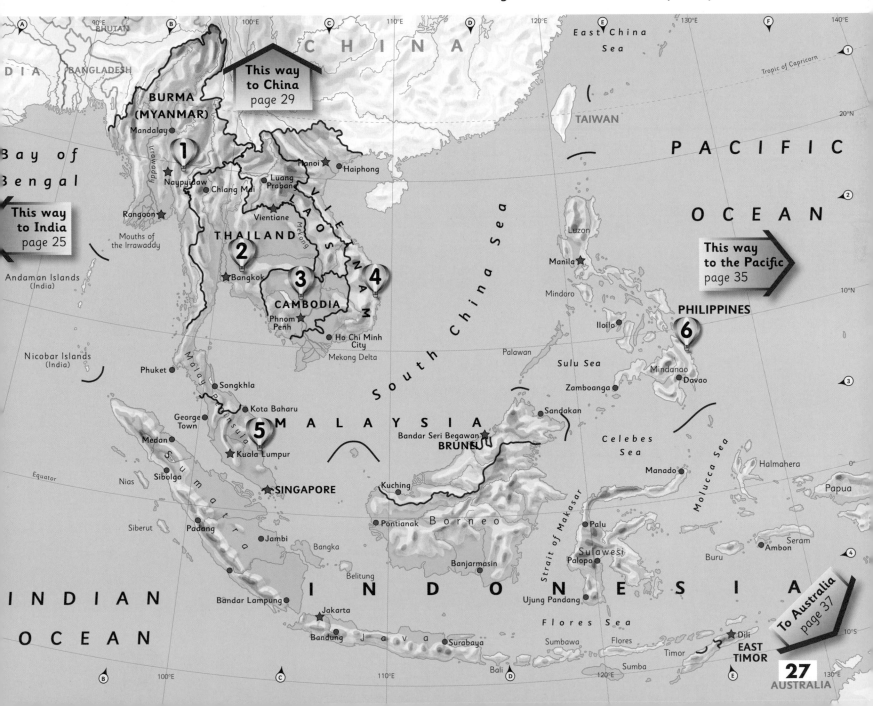

CHINA

This way to China page 29

East China Sea

BHUTAN

DIA   BANGLADESH

BURMA (MYANMAR)

Mandalay

Irrawaddy

1

Naypyidaw   Chiang Mai

Bay of Bengal

Hanoi   Haiphong

Luang Prabang

Rangoon

Vientiane

This way to India page 25

Mouths of the Irrawaddy

THAILAND

Andaman Islands (India)

2

Bangkok

3

CAMBODIA

Phnom Penh

4

Ho Chi Minh City

Mekong Delta

Nicobar Islands (India)

Phuket

Songkhla

South China Sea

TAIWAN

PACIFIC OCEAN

Tropic of Capricorn

20°N

Luzon

Manila

Mindoro

This way to the Pacific page 35

10°N

PHILIPPINES

Iloilo

Palawan

6

Sulu Sea

Mindanao

Davao

Zamboanga   Sandakan

Malay Peninsula

George Town

Kota Baharu

5   MALAYSIA

Medan

Kuala Lumpur

Sumatra

Equator   Nias   Sibolga

SINGAPORE

Kuching

Bandar Seri Begawan

BRUNEI

Celebes Sea

Manado

Halmahera

Papua

Siberut   Padang

Jambi

Bangka

Borneo

Pontianak

Strait of Makasar

Palu

Sulawesi

Palopo

Buru

Seram

Ambon

Molucca Sea

Banjarmasin

Belitung

INDONESIA

INDIAN OCEAN

Bandar Lampung

Jakarta

Bandung   Java

Surabaya

Ujung Pandang

Flores Sea

Sumbawa   Flores

Bali   Sumba

Timor

To Australia page 37

EAST TIMOR

Dili

Discover...
China and its Neighbours

1 The Bactrian camel (Asian camel) has **two humps** and can live in dry places that are hot or cold. A few wild camels still live in **Mongolia**.

2 **An army made of clay!** The Terracotta Army was made over 2,000 years ago. It was buried with the Emperor of Quin, who believed he would need an army in the after-life. There are over **8,000 figures** of men and horses! Each one is different, and they are as big as real people!

3 These children in China are learning **Kung Fu.** Children all over the world learn martial arts that came from Eastern Asia. **Kung Fu** – from China; **Karate** – from Japan; **Tae kwon do** – from Korea.

4 **China has many big cities** with big buildings and factories where lots of people live and work. Lots of things are made in China and sold all over the world.

6 **Japan has beautiful old palaces**, and flowering cherry trees in spring.

5

North Korea flag

Korea is split into 2 countries: North Korea and South Korea.

South Korea flag

Scale 1:25,000,000 1 cm on the map = 250 km on the ground

| 0 | 250 km | 500 km | 1,000 km | 1,500 km | 2,000 km | 2,500 km | 3,000 km |

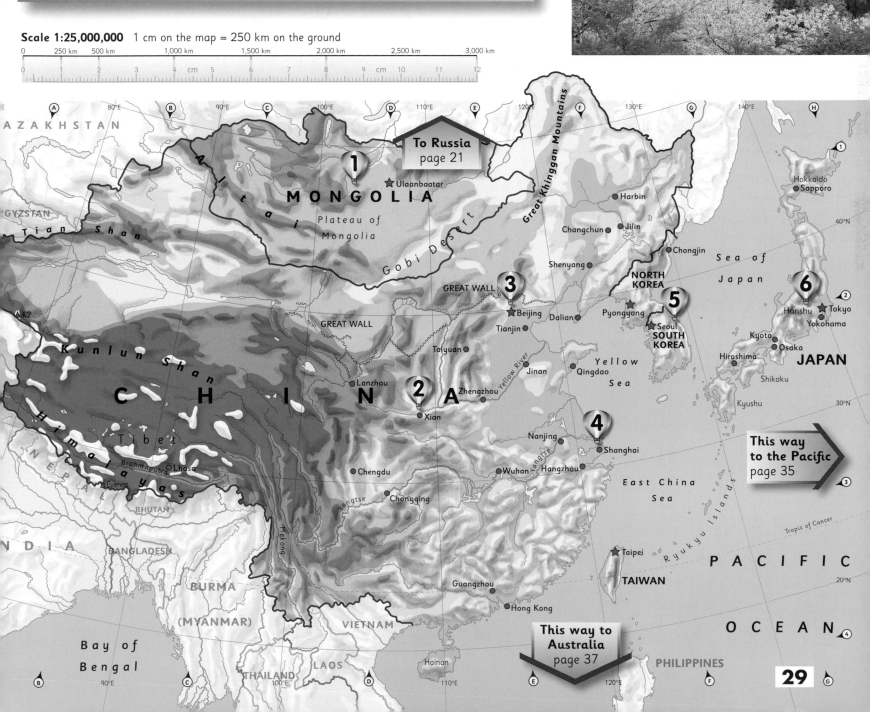

AZAKHSTAN

GYZSTAN

Tian Shan

Altai

MONGOLIA
Plateau of Mongolia

Gobi Desert

Great Khinggan Mountains

★ Ulaanbaatar

1

To Russia
page 21

Harbin

Changchun ● Jilin

Shenyang ●

Chongjin

Sea of Japan

Hokkaido
● Sapporo

40°N

K2

Kunlun Shan

Himalaya's

Tibet

Everest ○ Lhasa

Brahmaputra

NEPAL

BHUTAN

N D I A

BANGLADESH

C   H   I   N   A

GREAT WALL

GREAT WALL

Lanzhou ○

3
★ Beijing

Tianjin ○

Taiyuan ○

Yellow River

Zhengzhou ○

2
○ Xian

Jinan ○

Dalian ○

Qingdao ○

Yellow Sea

NORTH KOREA

Pyongyang ★

5

Seoul ★
SOUTH KOREA

Hiroshima ○

Honshu

6
★ Tokyo
Yokohama

Kyoto ○
Osaka ○

JAPAN

Shikoku

Kyushu

30°N

Chengdu ●

Chongqing ○

Nanjing ○

Wuhan ○ Hangzhou ○

4
○ Shanghai

Yangtze

Mekong

Yangtse

East China Sea

This way to the Pacific
page 35

Ryukyu Islands

Tropic of Cancer

BURMA
(MYANMAR)

Bay of Bengal

THAILAND

LAOS

VIETNAM

Guangzhou ●

● Hong Kong

Hainan

TAIWAN
★ Taipei

P A C I F I C

20°N

PHILIPPINES

O C E A N

This way to Australia
page 37

80°E   90°E   100°E   110°E   120°E   130°E   140°E

90°E   100°E   110°E   120°E

Discover...
North and West Africa

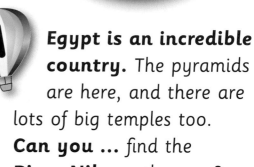

Egypt is an incredible country. The pyramids are here, and there are lots of big temples too. **Can you ...** find the **River Nile** on the map?

An oasis in the desert. Deserts are so dry that hardly any people, animals or plants can live there. But where there is **water** there is life.

A ruined Roman city in Libya. There are lots of ruins like this. The cities were built by the Romans over 2,000 years ago. The land here used to be good for farming. Wheat was then sent back to Rome.

What makes a camel so good at living in deserts? Their **thick fur** keeps camels cool in the day and warm at night. Their **wide feet** stop them sinking into loose sand and stones. Their **nostrils** shut so sand cannot blow in. And they can last a long time with **no water**!

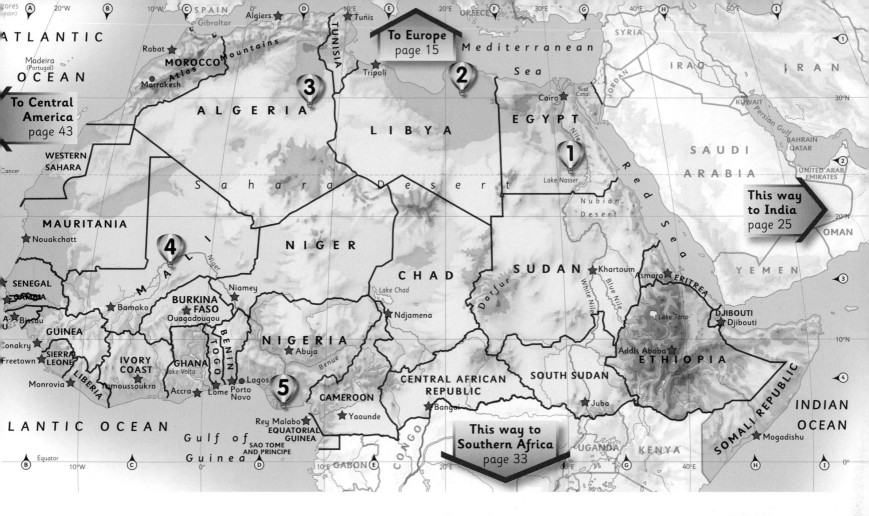

ATLANTIC OCEAN

Madeira (Portugal)

To Central America
page 43

To Europe
page 15

Mediterranean Sea

SPAIN
Gibraltar
Algiers
Tunis
Rabat
MOROCCO
Atlas Mountains
Marrakesh
Tripoli

3

ALGERIA

2

LIBYA

GREECE

SYRIA
IRAQ
IRAN

Cairo
Suez Canal
JORDAN
KUWAIT
Persian Gulf

EGYPT

1

Lake Nasser

SAUDI ARABIA

BAHRAIN
QATAR
UNITED ARAB EMIRATES

This way to India
page 25

OMAN

WESTERN SAHARA
Cancer

Sahara Desert

Nubian Desert

Red Sea

YEMEN

MAURITANIA
Nouakchott

4

MALI

NIGER

CHAD

SUDAN
Khartoum
Darfur
White Nile
Blue Nile
Asmara
ERITREA

DJIBOUTI
Djibouti

SENEGAL
GAMBIA
Bissau
GUINEA
Conakry
SIERRA LEONE
Freetown
LIBERIA
Monrovia

Bamako
Niamey
BURKINA FASO
Ouagadougou
BENIN
TOGO
GHANA
IVORY COAST
Yamoussoukro
Accra
Lome
Porto Novo

Niger

Lake Chad
Ndjamena

NIGERIA
Abuja
Benue

5

Lagos

CAMEROON
Yaounde

CENTRAL AFRICAN REPUBLIC
Bangui

SOUTH SUDAN
Juba

Lake Tana
Addis Ababa
ETHIOPIA

SOMALI REPUBLIC
Mogadishu

INDIAN OCEAN

ATLANTIC OCEAN

Equator

Gulf of Guinea

Rey Malabo
EQUATORIAL GUINEA
SAO TOME AND PRINCIPE

GABON
CONGO

This way to Southern Africa
page 33

UGANDA
KENYA

Scale 1:34,500,000   1 cm on the map = 345 km on the ground

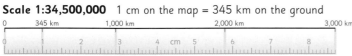

0   345 km   1,000 km   2,000 km   3,000 km

0   1   2   3   4   cm   5   6   7   8

4 **A village in Mali.** These women are preparing a meal. Here there is a rainy season and a dry season. In June it rains and crops grow, but December is very hot and dry.

5 **Oil and gas in Nigeria.** Oil and gas have made a few Nigerians rich. But many people are still very poor and **pollution** is a big problem. Nigeria has more people than any country in Europe.

Did you know?
This bird is called an **African jacana**. It lives in wet areas and its big feet allow it to walk over marshy land.

31

Discover...
Central and Southern Africa

1 **A baobab tree has such a fat trunk!** The long hot dry season is no problem for a baobab as it stores water in its amazing trunk! It is sometimes called an 'upside-down' tree because the fat stumpy branches look more like roots!

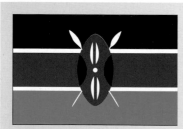

The flag of Kenya shows an African shield and 2 spears.
Black is for the African people.
Red is for the red blood of all people.
Green is for Kenya's rich agriculture.

2 **Coffee grows best where daytime is very hot and the nights are cold.** High land in Uganda is just right for growing good coffee beans!

3 **These stamps from Burundi** show a lion, a water buffalo, 2 hippos and a giraffe. Can you think of any other amazing animals in Africa?

Did you know?
There are 2 big long lakes in Africa – can you find them on the map?*
Long ago the land split apart, and this '**rift valley**' became deeper and wider.

4 **Elephants in the Namib Desert.**
Elephants are usually found on the grasslands but these live in the desert. Lions live here too!

5 **Johannesburg is a big city in South Africa.** Some hills are man-made: they are the waste rock from gold mines! The gold makes some people rich, but many people in Africa have very little money.

6 **SURPRISE!**
There are penguins on the south coast of South Africa – even though they are thousands of miles from Antarctica!

90c
Suid-Afrika
South Africa
DENIS MURPHY   SPHENISCUS DEMERSUS

To the rest of Africa page 31

This way to Australia page 37

To South America page 45

This way to Antarctica page 47

Map labels:
CAMEROON
EQUATORIAL GUINEA
Libreville
GABON
CONGO
Brazzaville
Kinshasa
CABINDA
Luanda
Congo Basin
DEMOCRATIC REPUBLIC OF THE CONGO
ANGOLA
SOUTH SUDAN
ETHIOPIA
Lake Turkana
UGANDA
KENYA
Kampala
Lake Victoria
Kigali
RWANDA
BURUNDI
Bujumbura
Nairobi
Mount Kenya
Mount Kilimanjaro
Mombasa
SOMALI REPUBLIC
Equator
INDIAN OCEAN
Seychelles
TANZANIA
Dodoma
Zanzibar
Lake Tanganyika
ZAMBIA
Lusaka
Zambezi
MALAWI
Lake Malawi
Lilongwe
MOZAMBIQUE
COMOROS
Moroni
Mayotte (France)
Mozambique Channel
MADAGASCAR
Antananarivo
Reunion (France)
Victoria Falls
Harare
ZIMBABWE
Limpopo
NAMIBIA
Windhoek
Namib Desert
BOTSWANA
Kalahari Desert
Gaborone
Pretoria
Johannesburg
Mbabane
SWAZILAND
Maputo
LESOTHO
Maseru
SOUTH AFRICA
Cape Town
Cape of Good Hope
ATLANTIC OCEAN
INDIAN OCEAN
Tropic of Capricorn

Scale 1:34,500,000 1 cm on the map = 345 km on the ground
345 km   1,000 km   2,000 km   3,000 km

Discover...
The Pacific

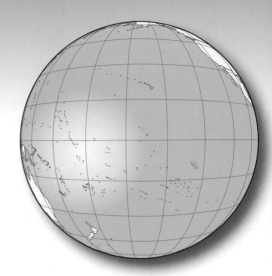

1 The Mariana Trench is the deepest part of the ocean anywhere in the world. Strange-looking creatures live in the deep ocean where daylight can never reach – like this one!

The Pacific is the biggest ocean in the world by far. It covers a third of the globe!

3 A Southern Cassowary – this large bird lives in the forests of New Guinea. But it cannot fly!

2 High islands are volcanoes. Volcanic soil is good for growing crops. But farmers must beware when a volcano is active, as it may erupt and send out lava.

Can you find these names on the maps?
Micronesia means 'little islands'.
Melanesia means 'black islands' – the sand is black from the volcanic rock.
Polynesia means 'lots of islands'.

4 Low islands are coral islands. The sand is white! People can live on these islands but flooding from the sea is a big worry. A **coral atoll** has calm sea in the centre, but round the edges of the atoll the sea is sometimes rough.

5 **Hawaii is the 50th state of the USA.**
Here in the Pacific Ocean the sea is deep and warm. Many visitors come to Hawaii to enjoy the surfing.

6 **Pacific islanders at work.**
This canoe has been **dug out** from **ONE** forest tree by these Pacific islanders.

Thousands of years ago people sailed in search of land in boats like these, using the stars to find their way.

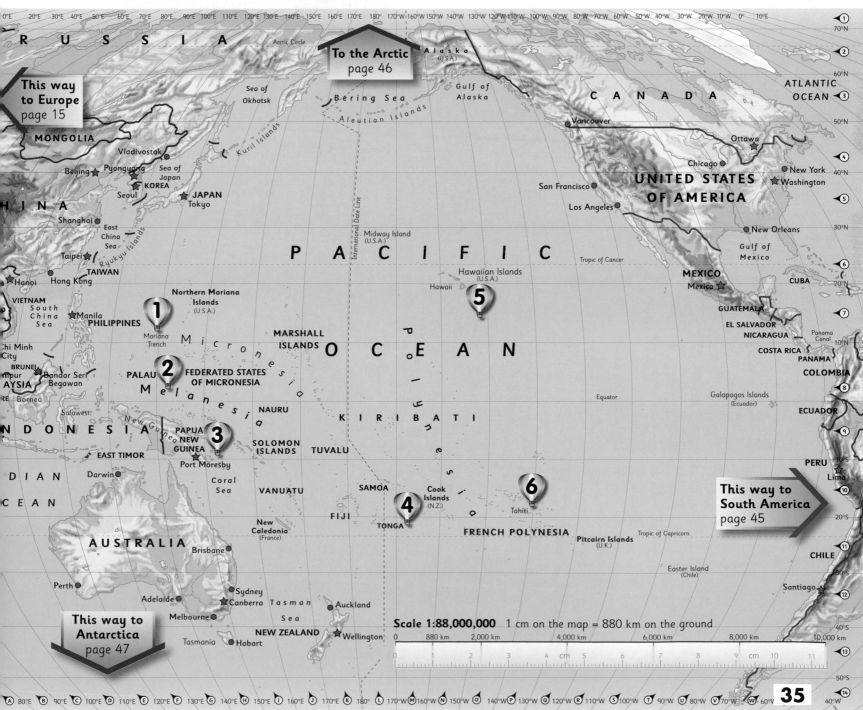

To the Arctic
page 46

This way
to Europe
page 15

This way to
South America
page 45

This way to
Antarctica
page 47

RUSSIA

Arctic Circle

Alaska (U.S.A.)

ATLANTIC OCEAN

Sea of Okhotsk

Bering Sea

Gulf of Alaska

CANADA

Aleutian Islands

MONGOLIA

Vladivostok

Kuril Islands

Vancouver

Ottawa

Beijing Pyongyang

Sea of Japan

Chicago

New York
Washington

KOREA

Seoul

JAPAN
Tokyo

San Francisco

UNITED STATES
OF AMERICA

Shanghai

East China Sea

Los Angeles

HINA

New Orleans

Taipei

Ryukyu Islands

Gulf of Mexico

Hanoi   Hong Kong

TAIWAN

P A C I F I C

Hawaiian Islands (U.S.A.)

Tropic of Cancer

MEXICO

CUBA

Hawaii

Mexico

VIETNAM
South China Sea

Manila

PHILIPPINES

Northern Mariana Islands (U.S.A.)

5

GUATEMALA

EL SALVADOR

Panama Canal

Chi Minh City

Mariana Trench

M i c r o n e s i a

MARSHALL ISLANDS

O C E A N

NICARAGUA

COSTA RICA

PANAMA

BRUNEI
mpur Bandar Seri Begawan

2

PALAU

FEDERATED STATES OF MICRONESIA

COLOMBIA

AYSIA

M e l a n e s i a

P o l y n e s i a

Equator

Galapagos Islands (Ecuador)

RE Borneo

Sulawesi

NAURU

K I R I B A T I

ECUADOR

N D O N E S I A

New Guinea

3

PAPUA NEW GUINEA

SOLOMON ISLANDS

TUVALU

Port Moresby

PERU

Lima

DIAN

Darwin

Coral Sea

VANUATU

SAMOA

Cook Islands (N.Z.)

6

This way to
South America
page 45

CEAN

EAST TIMOR

4

Tahiti

AUSTRALIA

New Caledonia (France)

FIJI

TONGA

FRENCH POLYNESIA

Pitcairn Islands (U.K.)

Tropic of Capricorn

CHILE

Brisbane

Easter Island (Chile)

Perth

Santiago

Adelaide

Sydney

Canberra

Tasman

Auckland

Melbourne

Sea

NEW ZEALAND Wellington

Tasmania Hobart

Midway Island (U.S.A.)

International Date Line

Scale 1:88,000,000   1 cm on the map = 880 km on the ground

0   880 km   2,000 km   4,000 km   6,000 km   8,000 km   10,000 km

0   1   2   3   4 cm 5   6   7   8   9 cm 10   11

A 80°E B 90°E C 100°E D 110°E E 120°E F 130°E G 140°E H 150°E I 160°E J 170°E K 180° L 170°W M 160°W N 150°W O 140°W P 130°W Q 120°W R 110°W S 100°W T 90°W U 80°W V 70°W W 60°W   40°W

35

Discover...
Australia and New Zealand

1 **Lots of trees in Australia are eucalyptus (gum) trees.** The hot dry climate means forest fires are often a problem, but gum trees are the first to grow back. They can take over the land from other plants, because they are quicker to grow again.

Australia has some amazing animals. Platypuses are mammals, but lay eggs. The **koala** is good at climbing gum trees to eat the leaves. Koalas have finger prints that look like human finger prints!

2 **Aborigines have lived in Australia for a very long time.** They learned to make all they needed from the land, plants and animals. This man is playing a **'didgeridoo'** – it is a musical instrument made from a long hollow branch.

3 **The Great Barrier Reef is the biggest coral reef in the world.** Visitors love to see the wonderful sea life by scuba-diving or looking through a glass-bottomed boat.

4 **Melbourne is the main city of the state of Victoria.** Australia has 7 states – can you find them on the map? All the biggest cities of Australia are near the sea.

Australia	New Zealand

SURPRISE! There's a flag from page 13 on these flags! The stars show the 'Southern Cross'. Can you see the differences?*

5 **Kiwis live in New Zealand.** These birds do not fly but come out at night and look for grubs to eat.

Can you find fruit from New Zealand? Look in shops for the labels.

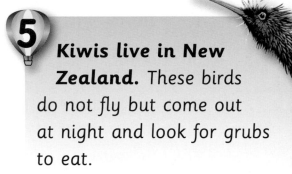

Zespri GREEN 4030 NEW ZEALAND

NEW ZEALAND BRAEBURN #4101

ROYAL GALA 4173 PickMee! New Zealand

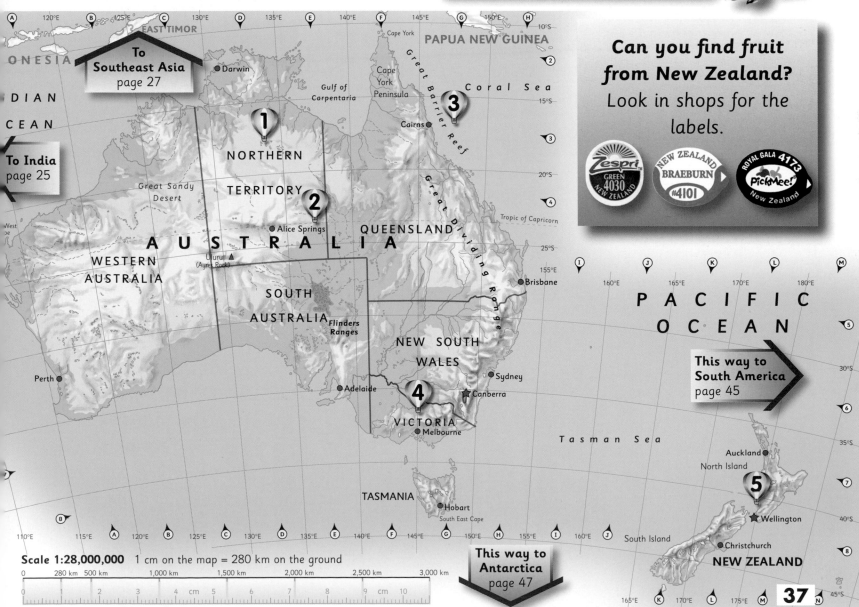

EAST TIMOR

To Southeast Asia page 27

●Darwin

PAPUA NEW GUINEA

Cape York

ONESIA

DIAN

CEAN

To India page 25

Gulf of Carpentaria

Cape York Peninsula

Coral Sea

●Cairns

15°S

1

3

NORTHERN

Great Sandy Desert

TERRITORY

2

20°S

●Alice Springs

QUEENSLAND

Tropic of Capricorn

25°S

A U S T R A L I A

Uluru ▲ (Ayres Rock)

WESTERN AUSTRALIA

SOUTH

AUSTRALIA Flinders Ranges

NEW SOUTH

WALES

●Brisbane

155°E

160°E

165°E

170°E

180°E

P A C I F I C

O C E A N

Perth ●

●Sydney

●Adelaide

4

★Canberra

This way to South America page 45

30°S

VICTORIA

●Melbourne

T a s m a n S e a

35°S

Auckland●

North Island

TASMANIA

●Hobart

South East Cape

South Island

Wellington

40°S

5

●Christchurch

Scale 1:28,000,000 1 cm on the map = 280 km on the ground

0   280 km 500 km   1,000 km   1,500 km   2,000 km   2,500 km   3,000 km

This way to Antarctica page 47

NEW ZEALAND

37

Discover... Canada and Alaska

1 **Alaska has amazing wildlife, like this Alaskan grizzly bear.** Alaska is part of the USA: the USA bought it from Russia in 1867. It is near Russia and partly in the Arctic. In winter it is very cold and days are short.

Do you know any Native American words?
Canada means 'village' in Mohawk.
Kayak is a boat like a canoe.
Wigwam and **Teepee**: these are types of tent.

2 **There is oil in Alaska.** This is an oil terminal on the Alaskan coast. Can you see 2 big tankers (ships)?

3 **This train travels right across Canada, over plains and mountains.** This picture shows the Rocky Mountains. Canada is the second biggest country in the world. It takes 4 days for a train to travel from one side to the other!

RUSSIA

ARCTIC OCEAN

GREENLAND
(Denmark)

ICELAND

To the North Pole
page 46

Bering Strait

Beaufort Sea

Queen Elizabeth Islands

McClure Strait

Ellesmere Island

Baffin Bay

Davis Strait

Denmark Strait

ATLANTIC OCEAN

Arctic Circle

Yukon

Alaska
(USA)

Mount McKinley

Alaska Range

Anchorage

Gulf of Alaska

This way to Asia
page 29

PACIFIC OCEAN

Whitehorse

YUKON TERRITORY

NORTHWEST TERRITORIES

Yellowknife

Victoria Island

NUNAVUT

Hudson Strait

Hudson Bay

This way to Europe
page 15

Labrador Sea

NEWFOUNDLAND AND LABRADOR

Labrador

Labrador City

Look at the map. Can you see the Rocky Mountains stretching down the western side of Canada and into the USA?

Skagway

Alaska Peninsula

BRITISH COLUMBIA

Fraser

Vancouver Island

Victoria

Vancouver

Rocky Mountains

ALBERTA

Calgary

C A N A D A

SASKATCHEWAN

Regina

Winnipeg

MANITOBA

Lake Winnipeg

ONTARIO

Lake Superior

QUEBEC

St Lawrence

Quebec

Montreal

Ottawa

Fredericton

NEW BRUNSWICK

Gulf of St Lawrence

PRINCE EDWARD ISLAND

St John's
Newfoundland

NOVA SCOTIA

Halifax

Cape Sable

ATLANTIC OCEAN

Toronto

Lake Huron

Lake Michigan

Lake Ontario

Niagara Falls

Lake Erie

UNITED STATES OF AMERICA

Scale 1:30,000,000 1 cm on the map = 300 km on the ground

0 300 km 1,000 km 1,500 km 2,000 km 2,500 km 3,000 km 3,500 km

0 1 2 3 4 cm 5 6 7 8 9 cm 10 11

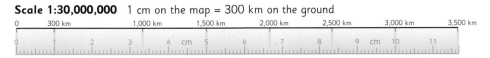

The Canadian flag has a red maple leaf on it. In autumn the maple leaves turn red. Some people say the hills turn red like fire.

The Niagara Falls are shared by Canada and the USA.
They are between Lake Erie and Lake Ontario.

5 Newfoundland was named when Europeans 'found' it. This fishing village is **MUCH** closer to Europe than to western Canada!

39

Discover...
The USA

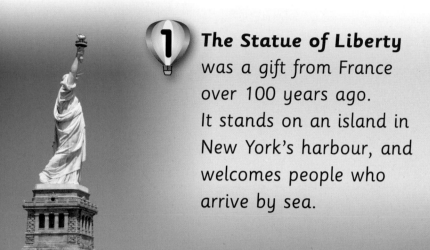

1 **The Statue of Liberty** was a gift from France over 100 years ago. It stands on an island in New York's harbour, and welcomes people who arrive by sea.

The bald eagle – America's national bird. This eagle is not really bald! The feathers on its head are pure white. It feeds on fish, mainly salmon.

3 **Monument Valley**. These amazing sandstone formations are in the Arizona desert. They are **huge**! Can you see a car at the bottom of the picture?

2 **Harvesting wheat**. Large machines called combine harvesters, like the red one in this picture, are used to harvest the grain.

Can you . . . find a long river with a long name on the map?* Here's a clue: •ISS•SSI••I

(Hint!)↑

5 A tram station in downtown San Diego.
Trams are a great way to travel in cities: they travel fast on rails and they are clean and quiet.

4 **The oldest living thing on Earth?**
Bristlecone pine trees live for a very long time. Some of them are about 5,000 years old.

Did you know?
The names of states tell us about the origins of the peoples of America:
Vermont – means 'green mountain' (French).
Nevada – means 'snowy' (Spanish).
Iowa – means 'beautiful land' (American Indian).

Scale 1:21,500,000 1 cm on the map = 215 km on the ground

0   215 km   500 km   1,000 km   1,500 km   2,000 km   2,500 km

0   1   2   3   4 cm 5   6   7   8   9 cm 10   11

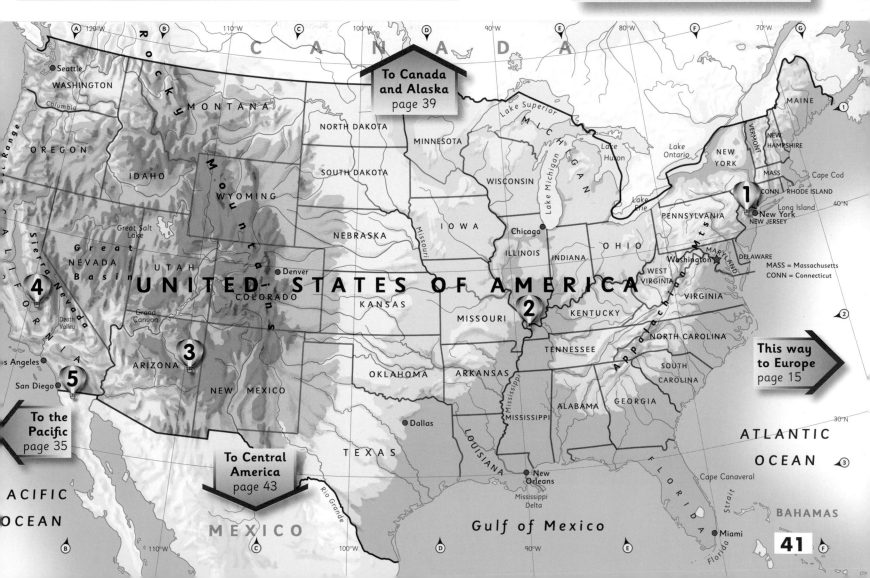

To Canada and Alaska page 39

This way to Europe page 15

To the Pacific page 35

To Central America page 43

MASS = Massachusetts
CONN = Connecticut

UNITED STATES OF AMERICA

Discover... Central America

1 **Mexico is a big country. Mexico City** is one of the biggest and busiest cities in the world. There are big deserts, mountains and volcanoes in Mexico.

2 **This rare bird lives in the rainforests of Central America.** It is a **quetzal**. A lot of the wildlife in the forests is very special, so it is important to look after the forests for the wildlife.

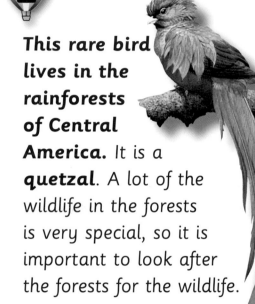

NORTH AMERICA
Atlantic Ocean
Panama Canal
Pacific Ocean
SOUTH AMERICA

4 **The flag of Jamaica:**
Green – for farming
Gold – for sunshine
Black – for hardship

3 **The Panama Canal is amazing – and useful too!** Big ships can go from the **Pacific Ocean** to the **Atlantic Ocean**. How do you think ships could get from the Pacific to the Atlantic Ocean before this canal was dug?* Do you think it took a long time? The globe will help you!

6 **A carnival procession on Curaçao.** These women are enjoying a colourful street carnival. **SURPRISE!** Curaçao is a **Dutch** island.

Maize first came from Central America. Now it is grown all over the world. As well as corn-on-the-cob and sweetcorn, it is used for cornflakes and popcorn, and its flour is used in tortillas.

5 **So many islands!** Tourists can travel on a ship and visit one island every day in the Caribbean. But beware of **hurricanes**!

Bananas grow fast. This stamp shows bananas growing. Look hard at the stamp .... **Can you see** the green bananas growing – upwards?

Scale 1:26,500,000 1cm on the map = 265 km on the ground

| 0 | 265km | 1,000km | 1,500km | 2,000km | 2,500km | 3,000km | 3,500km |

0 1 2 3 4 cm 5 6 7 8 9 10 11 12 13cm

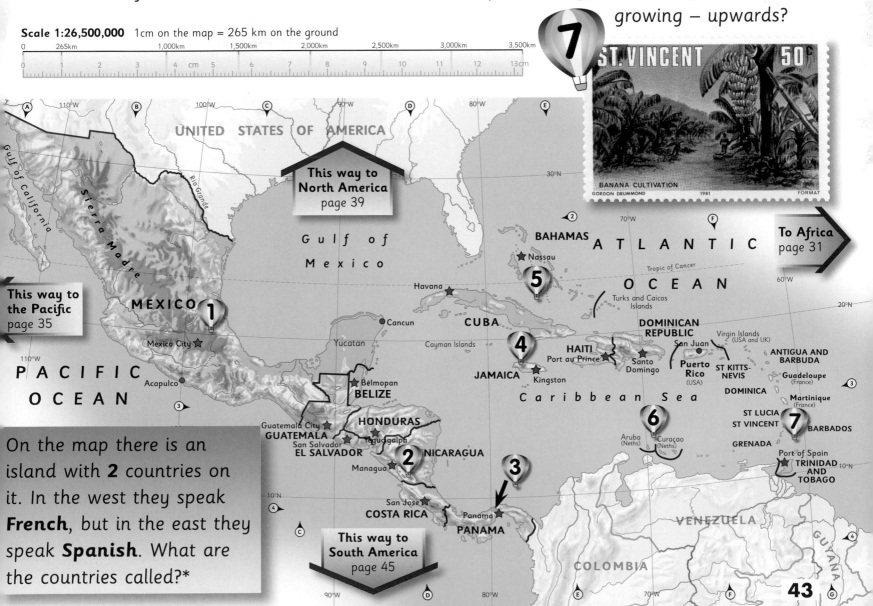

7 ST. VINCENT 50c

BANANA CULTIVATION
GORDON DRUMMOND 1981 FORMAT

This way to **North America** page 39

This way to the Pacific page 35

To Africa page 31

On the map there is an island with **2** countries on it. In the west they speak **French**, but in the east they speak **Spanish**. What are the countries called?*

This way to **South America** page 45

UNITED STATES OF AMERICA

Gulf of California

Sierra Madre

Rio Grande

Gulf of Mexico

MEXICO **1**

Mexico City

Acapulco

PACIFIC OCEAN

Cancun

Yucatan

Guatemala City
GUATEMALA
San Salvador
EL SALVADOR

Belmopan
BELIZE

HONDURAS
Tegucigalpa

Managua

NICARAGUA **2**

San Jose
COSTA RICA

Panama
PANAMA **3**

Havana

CUBA

Cayman Islands

JAMAICA
Kingston **4**

BAHAMAS
Nassau **5**

Tropic of Cancer

Turks and Caicos Islands

HAITI
Port au Prince

DOMINICAN REPUBLIC
Santo Domingo

San Juan
Puerto Rico
(USA)

Virgin Islands
(USA and UK)

ST KITTS-NEVIS

ANTIGUA AND BARBUDA

Guadeloupe (France)

DOMINICA

Martinique (France)

ST LUCIA
ST VINCENT **7** BARBADOS

GRENADA

Port of Spain
TRINIDAD AND TOBAGO

Caribbean Sea

Aruba (Neths)
Curaçao (Neths) **6**

ATLANTIC OCEAN

VENEZUELA

COLOMBIA

GUYANA

43

Discover...
South America

1 **A giant tortoise on the Galapagos Islands.** These volcanic islands are very far from other land. As a result, many special animals and plants only live here. **Can you** guess the age of the oldest giant tortoise?*

3 **Lake Titicaca is high up in the Andes**. These boats are made from reeds (surprise!), and they do float. It is so high up here that visitors get out of breath. **Can you** see which **2** countries share the lake?*

2 **The Amazon jungle is hot and wet.** The river is called the Amazon too! The trees are very big. There are so many different animals and plants here that no-one has ever seen them all. But some of the jungle is being chopped down.

4 **Buenos Aires.** This is the capital city of a big country — can you find it on the map?* 'Buenos Aires' means 'good air' in Spanish.

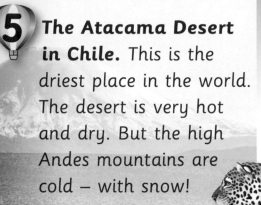

5 **The Atacama Desert in Chile.** This is the driest place in the world. The desert is very hot and dry. But the high Andes mountains are cold – with snow!

Which is the biggest cat in South America? It is the **jaguar**! Most jaguars live in the lowland rainforests near the Amazon River.

6 This is a '**monkey puzzle tree**'. It grows in the south of Chile – its real name is a '**Chilean pine**'. **Is it chilly in Chile?** Sometimes! It is cold in the high mountains and in the south of Chile. But it is hot in the desert and in the summer (December) in central Chile.

Can you find how many countries touch Brazil?*

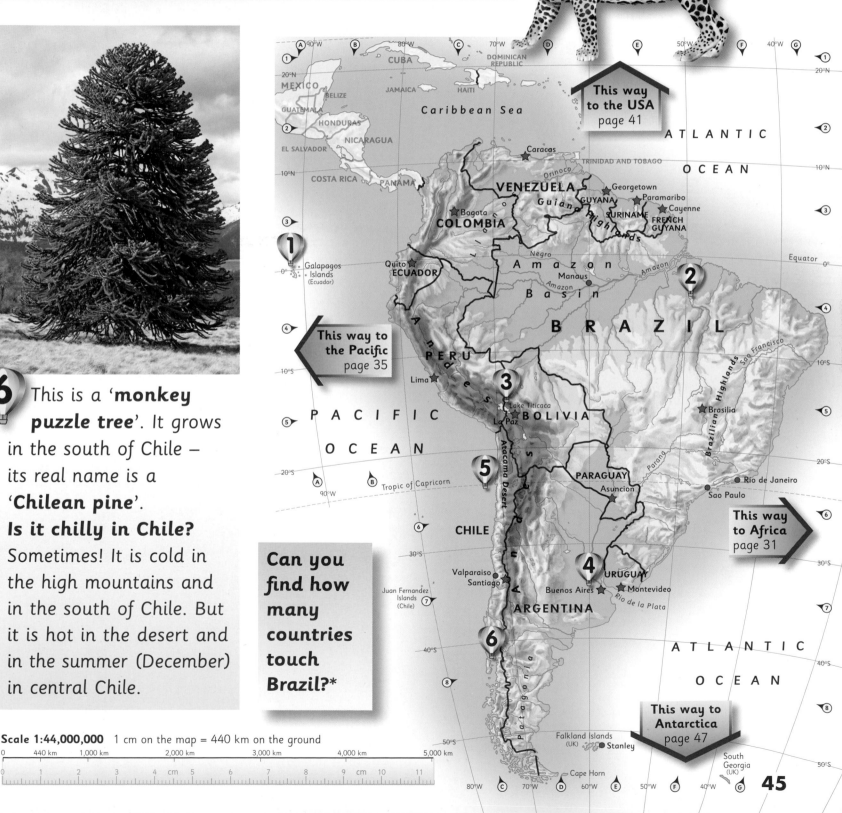

This way to the USA page 41

This way to the Pacific page 35

This way to Africa page 31

This way to Antarctica page 47

Scale 1:44,000,000   1 cm on the map = 440 km on the ground

0   440 km   1,000 km   2,000 km   3,000 km   4,000 km   5,000 km

0   1   2   3   4   cm 5   6   7   8   9   cm 10   11

Discover...
The Arctic

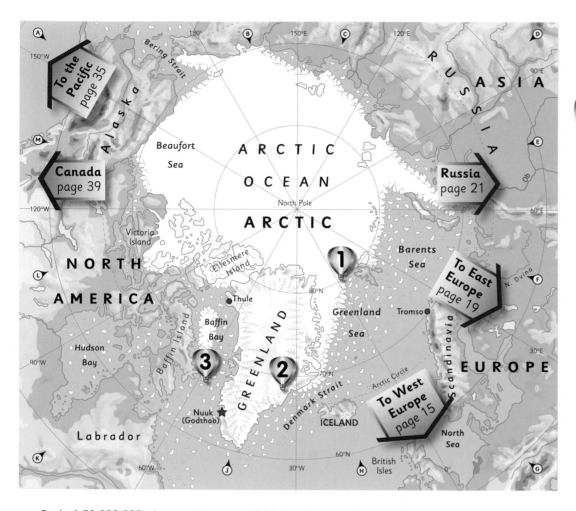

Scale 1:50,000,000   1 cm on the map = 500 km on the ground

| 0 | 500 km | 1,000 km | 2,000 km | 4,000 km | 6,000 km | 8,000 km | 10,000 km |

Greenland is mostly white with ice, not green! These owls are white so they are hard to see in the snow.

AMAZING! In the **ARCTIC**, there are 24 hours of **daylight** in **June** and 24 hours of **darkness** in **December**.

1 Polar bears live in the Arctic. They are the biggest of all the bears. They hunt for fish and seals.

3 People live in the Arctic. This Inuit hunter and his dogsled team are travelling on the frozen polar sea of Baffin Bay.

Discover...
Antarctica

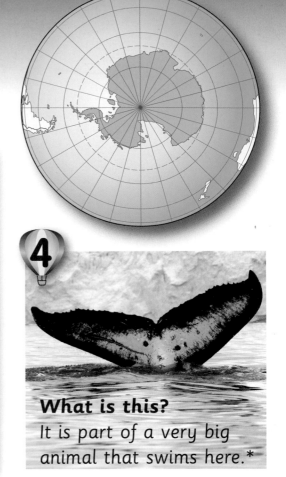

1 **Penguins live in the Antarctic**. They can't fly but they are brilliant swimmers.

AMAZING! In the **ANTARCTIC**, there are 24 hours of **darkness** in **June** and 24 hours of **daylight** in **December**.

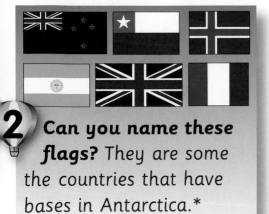

2 **Can you name these flags?** They are some the countries that have bases in Antarctica.*

3 **Some tourists come to see Antarctica by boat.** Beware of icebergs!

4

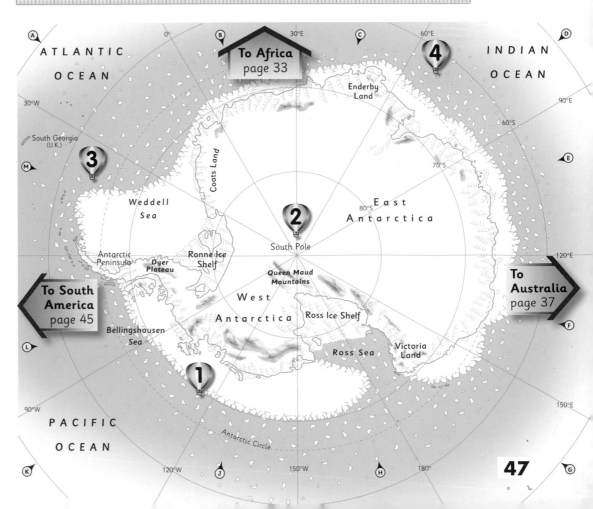

What is this? It is part of a very big animal that swims here.*

Scale 1:50,000,000   1 cm on the map = 500 km on the ground

| 0 | 500 km | 1,000 km | 2,000 km | 4,000 km | 6,000 km | 8,000 km | 10,000 km |

0 1 2 3 4 cm 5 6 7 8 9 cm 10 11 12

ATLANTIC OCEAN

To Africa page 33

INDIAN OCEAN

Enderby Land

South Georgia (U.K.)

Coats Land

Weddell Sea

East Antarctica

South Pole

Antarctic Peninsula   Dyer Plateau   Ronne Ice Shelf

Queen Maud Mountains

West Antarctica   Ross Ice Shelf

To South America page 45

Bellingshausen Sea

Victoria Land

Ross Sea

To Australia page 37

PACIFIC OCEAN

Antarctic Circle

Index

A
Afghanistan 25
Albania 17
Algeria 31
Angola 33
Antarctica 47
Antigua 43
Arabian Sea 23
Arctic 46
Argentina 45
Armenia 21
Atlantic Ocean 10
Australia 37
Austria 15
Azerbaijan 21
B
Bahamas 43
Bahrain 23
Baltic Sea 19
Bangladesh 25
Barbados 43
Belarus 19
Belgium 15
Belize 43
Benin 31
Bhutan 25
Black Sea 19
Bolivia 45
Bosnia 17
Botswana 33
Brazil 45
Brunei 27
Bulgaria 19
Burkina Faso 31
Burma 27
Burundi 33

C
Cambodia 27
Cameroon 31
Canada 39
Caribbean Sea 43
Caspian Sea 21
Central African Rep. 31
Chad 31
Chile 45
China 29
Colombia 45
Congo 33
Corsica 17
Costa Rica 43
Croatia 17
Cuba 43
Cyprus 23
Czech Republic 19
D
Denmark 15
Djibouti 31
Dominica 43
Dominican Republic 43
E
Easter Island 35
East Timor 27
Ecuador 45
Egypt 31
El Salvador 43
England 13
Equatorial Guinea 31
Eritrea 31
Estonia 19
Ethiopia 31
F
Falkland Islands 45

Fiji 35
Finland 15
France 15
G
Gabon 33
Galapagos Islands 45
Gambia 31
Georgia 21
Germany 15
Ghana 31
Greece 17
Greenland 46
Grenada 43
Guatemala 43
Guinea 31
Guinea Bissau 31
Gulf of Mexico 43
Guyana 45
H
Haiti 43
Hawaii 35
Honduras 43
Hungary 19
I
Iceland 15, 46
India 25
Indian Ocean 11
Indonesia 27, 35
Iran 23
Iraq 23
Ireland 13, 15
Israel 23
Italy 17
Ivory Coast 31
J
Jamaica 43
Japan 29, 35
Jordan 23
K
Kazakhstan 21
Kenya 33

Kiribati 35
Kosovo 19
Kuwait 23
Kyrgyzstan 21
L
Laos 27
Latvia 19
Lebanon 23
Lesotho 33
Liberia 31
Libya 31
Lithuania 19
Luxembourg 15
M
Macedonia 17, 19
Madagascar 33
Malawi 33
Malaysia 27
Maldives 25
Mali 31
Malta 17
Mauritania 31
Mediterranean Sea 17
Mexico 43
Moldova 19
Mongolia 29
Montenegro 17
Morocco 31
Mozambique 33
Myanmar 27
N
Namibia 33
Nauru 35
Nepal 25
Netherlands 15
New Zealand 37
Nicaragua 43
Niger 31
Nigeria 31
North Korea 29
North Pole 46

North Sea 15
Norway 15
O
Oman 23
P
Pacific Ocean 35
Pakistan 25
Panama 43
Papua New Guinea 35
Paraguay 45
Peru 45
Philippines 27, 35
Poland 19
Portugal 17
Puerto Rico 43
Q
Qatar 23
R
Red Sea 23, 31
Romania 19
Russia 21
Rwanda 33
S
Samoa 35
Sao Tome 31
Saudi Arabia 23
Scandinavia 46
Scotland 13
Senegal 31
Serbia 19
Seychelles 33
Sierra Leone 31
Singapore 27
Slovak Republic 19
Slovenia 17
Somali Republic 31
South Africa 33
South Korea 29
South Pole 47
South Sudan 31
Spain 17

Sri Lanka 25
St Kitts-Nevis 43
St Lucia 43
St Vincent 43
Sudan 31
Suriname 45
Swaziland 33
Sweden 15
Switzerland 15
Syria 23
T
Taiwan 29
Tajikistan 21
Tanzania 33
Thailand 27
Togo 31
Tonga 35
Trinidad and Tobago 43
Tunisia 31
Turkey 23
Turkmenistan 21
Tuvalu 35
U
Uganda 33
Ukraine 19
United Arab Emirates 23
United Kingdom 15
USA 41
Uruguay 45
Uzbekistan 21
V
Venezuela 45
Vietnam 27
W
Wales 13
Western Sahara 31
Y
Yemen 23
Z
Zambia 33
Zimbabwe 33

Answers to Questions

Page 10 USA, Brazil and Nigeria.

Page 19 New countries are Estonia, Latvia, Lithuania, Belarus, Ukraine, Moldova, Czech Republic, Slovak Republic, Slovenia, Croatia, Bosnia, Serbia, Montenegro, Kosovo, Macedonia. 2 big seas are Baltic and Black.

Page 21 The Caspian Sea is shared by Russia, Kazakhstan, Turkmenistan, Azerbaijan and Iran.

Page 22 The three continents are Africa, Asia and Europe.

Page 23 The biggest country is Saudi Arabia. The stamp shows 2 palm trees, 3 fruit trees, farmland, a village and a tower.

Page 33 Lake Tanganyika and Lake Malawi.

Page 37 Australia's flag has 6 stars. New Zealand's flag has 4 stars.

Page 40 Mississippi River.

Page 42 Ships had to go all the way around South America. See map on page 45.

Page 43 In Haiti the people speak French – in the Dominican Republic people speak Spanish.

Page 44 The oldest giant tortoise was 152 years old. Lake Titicaca is shared by Peru and Bolivia. Buenos Aires is the capital city of Argentina.

Page 45 10 countries touch Brazil.

Page 47 The flags are from New Zealand, Chile, Norway, Argentina, United Kingdom and France. The picture is of the tail of a whale.

Photo Acknowledgements

Robin Aiello (Ocean Antics Consulting) 36 centre bottom; **Alamy** /Ashley Cooper 13 top left, /David Lomax/Robert Harding Picture Library Ltd 14 top left, /Zaichiki 18 bottom left, /Bert de Ruiter 18 bottom right, /Iain Masterton 20 top right, /Oleg Moiseyenko 20 bottom left, /Dinodia Images 25 top left, /FAN travelstock 30 centre left, /Friedrich Stark 31 centre right, /Images&Stories 32 top left, /Images of Africa Photobank 31 top right, /Chad Ehlers 34 bottom, /Sami Sarkis Lifestyles 35 top right, /Terry Fincher.Photo Int 38 top right, /Images Etc Ltd 38 bottom, /blickwinkel 41 top left, /Ambient Images Inc. 41 top centre, /World Pictures 42 top left, /VI 43 top centre, /JUPITERIMAGES/Creatas 44 top left, /Mireille Vautier 44 bottom left, /Chad Ehlers 44 bottom right; **City of Johannesburg** / Walter Knirr 33 top right; **Corbis** /Comstock (RF) front-cover montage bottom, /Gabe Palmer/zefa 2 centre right, /Image Plan (RF) 6 montage top left, /Image100 (RF) 6 montage top right, /Robert Glusic (RF) 6 montage bottom left (and front-cover montage top), /Kristi J. Black (RF) 6 montage bottom right, /Pawel Libera 12 top left, /Felix Ordonez/Reuters 16 top left, / David Turnley 18 top left, /Kevin Burke 18 bottom centre, /Goodshoot 20 top right, /Atef Hassan/Reuters 22 bottom right, /Reuters 23 top left, /Paul Almasy 24 top left, /Steven Vidler/Eurasia Press 25 top right, /Jacques Langevin 28 top left, /Keren Su 28 centre right, /Yann Arthus-Bertrand 30 top left, /Bruno Fert 31 bottom left, /Image100 (RF) top left, /George Steinmetz 34 centre left, /Paul A. Souders 36 top left, /Claire Leimbach/ Robert Harding World Imagery 36 top right, /Erwin & Peggy Bauer/zefa 38 top left, /Danny Lehman 42 centre left, /DLILLC (RF) 46 bottom left, /Layne Kennedy 46 bottom right; **Dreamstime.com** /Gibbsterr 12 top right, / Railpix 12 bottom left, /Lastdays1 14 bottom left, /Kurt 14 bottom right, / Britvich 15 centre left, /Gnugent 17 centre left, /Dmitryp 20 bottom right, / Nalukai 35 top left, /Lesterlester 44 centre right, /Eg004713 45 bottom left, / Wildernessphotographs 45 centre left, /Bernardbreton 47 top left, /Cascoly 47 top centre; **Fotolia.com** /bobroy20 16 bottom right, /RadioUran 21 top left, /Alena Yakusheva 26 bottom left (and back cover), /Jorisvo 29 top left, /Stephan Karg 30 bottom centre, /robert paul van beets 37 top left; **Fugro NPA Ltd (www.fugro-npa.com)** 5 bottom, 8 top; **iStockphoto.com** /Rolf Weschke 13 top right, /Daniel Breckwoldt 15 top left, /Branislav Bubanja 16 bottom left, /Ricardo De Mattos 17 top left, / Angelafoto 17 top right, /Ferenc Vágvölgyi 19 bottom left, /Andrey Kolganov 20 centre, /Rob Broek 21 top right, /Steven Allan 22 top left, /Alena Yakusheva 22 bottom left, /David Ciemny 24 bottom left, /x-drew 24 bottom right, /Robert Churchill 26 bottom left, /Martyn Smith 26 bottom right, /Paolo Santoné 27 centre left, /Alan Tobey 28 bottom left, /Ralph Paprzycki 29 top right, /Richard Gunion 39 bottom centre, /Allan Morrison 39 bottom right, /Jeremy Edwards 40 top left, /Tony Campbell 40 centre left, / Steve Geer 43 top left, /Mark Fitzsimmons 47 top right; **NASA/GSFC** / Reto Stockli, Alan Nelson, Fritz Hasler 6 top; **Caroline Ohara** 40 bottom right; **Oxford Scientific (OSF)** /Paulo de Oliveira 34 top left.